ORPHEUS

ORPHEUS

RETOLD AND ILLUSTRATED BY
CHARLES MIKOLAYCAK

HARCOURT BRACE JOVANOVICH, PUBLISHERS

SAN DIEGO   NEW YORK   LONDON

HBJ

Copyright © 1992 by Charles Mikolaycak

Requests for permission to make copies of any part of the
work should be mailed to: Permissions Department,
Harcourt Brace Jovanovich, Publishers, 8th Floor,
Orlando, Florida 32887.

The song lyrics on pages 6, 14, 15, and 20 of this book were
adapted from Lionel Salter's 1987 English translation
of Alessandro Striggio's Italian libretto for Claudio
Monteverdi's 1607 opera, *L'Orfeo*.

Library of Congress Cataloging-in-Publication Data
Mikolaycak, Charles.
Orpheus/retold and illustrated by Charles Mikolaycak.
p.   cm.
Includes bibliographical references.
Summary: A retelling of the tragic myth of Orpheus
and his eternal love for the doomed Eurydice.
ISBN 0-15-258804-3
1. Orpheus (Greek mythology) — Juvenile literature. 2. Eurydice
(Greek mythology) — Juvenile literature. [1. Orpheus (Greek
mythology) 2. Eurydice (Greek mythology) 3. Mythology, Greek.]
I. Title.
BL820.O7M55   1992
398.21 — dc20   91-27440

First edition   A B C D E

The illustrations in this book were done with colored pencils,
watercolors, and acrylics on diazo prints made from pencil drawings.
The display type, based on Neuzeit Roman, was hand lettered
by Judythe Sieck.
The text type was set in Garamond No. 3 Bold by Thompson Type,
San Diego, California.
Color separations were made by Bright Arts, Ltd., Singapore.
Printed and bound by Tien Wah Press, Singapore
Production supervision by Warren Wallerstein and Ginger Boyer
Art direction by Michael Farmer
Designed by Charles Mikolaycak

To B.V. —
for hearing the music also
— C.M.

Sun, you who encircle and see all
From your celestial orbits,
Tell me, have you ever seen
A man more joyous and more fortunate than I?

So sang Orpheus. His music was so exquisite that mountains bowed and wild animals ceased their hunting to listen. The sea stopped spraying, and trees bent to better hear his songs.

When Orpheus sang, every heart opened. His melodies inspired the noblest love man and woman could hope for. His music was celebrated and cherished by all who heard it.

guided it back on course. Once, as Orpheus' ship navigated a dangerous coast, his fellow sailors became bewitched by the enchanted songs of the Sirens, temptresses who lured ships to their doom. Orpheus took up his lyre. When he began to sing, the Sirens' music lost all power to do harm and the women were changed into rocks. The ship continued its journey safely, and the warriors fought many battles, winning them all. Always they were inspired and comforted by the songs of Orpheus.

■

When the captain and crew returned victorious, Orpheus was rewarded for his heroic deeds. He was granted a treasure more precious than gems or a fine estate —

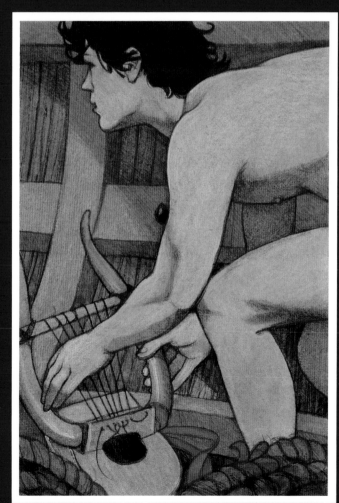

heart belonged to him.

They were married on a day when the sky was clear and flowers bloomed in celebration. Hymen, the god of marriage, stood nearby to bless them. A swirl of sparks, cinders, and black smoke spewed from his torch and darkened the sky. But Orpheus and Eurydice were too deeply in love to notice or fear this chilling omen from the gods.

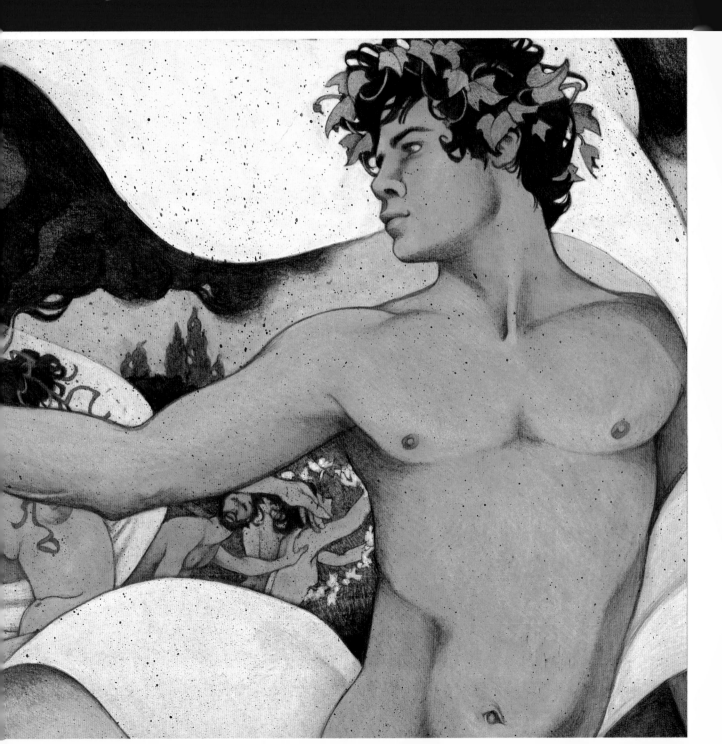

Their happiness was unequaled, yet it was destined to be brief. Soon after their wedding, Eurydice, gathering flowers, was approached by a jealous suitor. Refusing his declarations of love, she fled in terror. As she ran she stepped on a poisonous snake. When Orpheus found her, she was dead; her spirit had slipped away into the Underworld. Orpheus knelt by her side and wept.

For Orpheus, life without Eurydice was hopeless. A broken man, he took his lyre and wandered aimlessly, far from the land he had once brightened with joyous songs. Now he sang of despair, loss, loneliness.

You are dead, my life, yet I still breathe.
You have gone from me,
Never more to return, yet I remain.

The trees and stones, sea and sky, even the gods on Olympus were moved to tears by Orpheus' mournful songs. But no one in the Upper Air held enough power to grant new life to the dead. So Orpheus continued to

wander, sowing tears where he had once brought joy.

I will surely descend to the deepest abyss,
And having softened the heart of the King of Shadows,
I will bring Eurydice back with me to see the stars again.
Oh, if malign destiny denies me this,
I will remain with her in the company of death.
Farewell, earth. Farewell, sky. And sun, farewell.

At length, Orpheus came upon the cave leading to the Underworld. He knew that deep below, the gods King Hades and Queen Persephone ruled the spirits of the dead. Having lost all he cared for, Orpheus knew no fear and entered the cave. Soon he stood before the black waters of the River Styx. He sang of love and death, of the sweetness of the earth, and of the bitterness of losing what we hold most dear — for Orpheus was convinced that if the spirits felt his agony they would yield to his plea. Sure enough, his songs entranced the harsh ferryman, who forgot to ask for the coin he demanded from each soul crossing the river. Orpheus passed through the cave into the Underworld.

He traveled deeper into the silence until he reached the pool of Lethe, from which all souls entering the Underworld must drink. With one sip from this pool, all memory of life's pains and joys vanish. Yet even the spirits by the pool were enchanted by Orpheus' songs. These lifeless shades, enduring a thousand eternities in the Underworld, stopped and listened. Memories stirred in their hearts, and they wept. Even the Furies, the spirits who punished those who tampered with nature's laws, were moved to pity and grieved for Orpheus and his lost Eurydice. Tantalus paused in his efforts to quench his unbearable thirst, and Sisyphus ceased his endless attempts to roll his boulder uphill. A host of souls who had been cursed for eternity to perform impossible tasks were suddenly touched by the living sorrow of Orpheus' song.

Pushing deeper into the Underworld, Orpheus sang on. His gentle music reflected his longing for Eurydice, a love so powerful it had led him to this horrifying place. He begged the King and Queen to unite him with Eurydice once more.

Mighty spirits, fearsome deities,
Without whom no one can gain passage to
    the other shore,
Oh, hear me;
I am nothing.
Without my dear wife, how can it be that I am alive?

Queen Persephone sighed, remembering her own sweet secrets of life in the Upper Air. For a moment, even the King dreamt of life's pleasures. The yearning notes from Orpheus' lyre had kindled their memories, and so they summoned Eurydice to come forth. They would grant Orpheus' wish with one condition: he must not look at Eurydice until they reached the Upper Air. For if he glanced at her, even once, she would be swept back into the Underworld for eternity.

Out through the ragged caverns of darkness, Orpheus led Eurydice across black waters, through twilight, on toward the world of life. In ghostly silence, Eurydice followed, her steps making no sound. At last a shaft of

light pierced the cave. Orpheus, believing his agony had ended and anxious to see if Eurydice was with him, turned. But he turned too soon. Still in shadow and steps away from freedom, Eurydice was swept back into the Underworld, a forgiving smile on her lips.

Orpheus rushed to follow, but this time he was denied entrance. The ferryman offered no second chance, and as Orpheus groped in the darkness, the boatman carried Eurydice away.

Orpheus had no choice but to return to the Upper Air. For seven months he played his lyre beside the cave and sang of his woe. Neither the King nor the Queen of the Underworld took notice.

> What shall I do without Eurydice?
> Where shall I go without my love?
> Eurydice! Eurydice!
> Alas, there is no further help for me,
> No further hope on earth, nor yet in heaven.
> Oh, let my suffering cease
> Forever with my life.

So the sad pilgrimage of Orpheus began. He could no longer sing, for his was the silence that follows weeping. Mute with loss, he set off alone, empty of the joy that had once lifted his voice in song.

Early one morning, a crowd of revelers came upon him.

Despite his silence and worn appearance, they knew Orpheus at once. They respectfully asked him to play, but when he did not, they grew angry. Why did he refuse to play? Had he grown too proud, too fine to play his music for them? Their demands grew louder, but Orpheus was mute and remained still. He could not

sing. Someone threw a stone. Others followed with rocks. The crowd became a raging mob, and when it finally dispersed, Orpheus lay limp and bleeding.

Was it a relief then, when the crowd returned later, again demanding that he rise and play? For the lyre lay

silent beside the man whose spirit broke and scattered to the wind as the frenzied crowd descended upon him, ripping him limb from limb, casting his lyre and head into the river. Even in death, as he slipped below the water's surface, Orpheus opened his lips to call out the name of his beloved Eurydice again and again.

Quietly the people vanished; they too were destined to die, not today, but by degrees — and with memories they could not hope to understand. In the end nothing remained of the young musician and his songs of love for his dear wife. But the gods, in their wisdom, honored Orpheus and threw his lyre into the heavens, where it became a bright constellation of stars to tell his story and to shine on forever, for all eternity.

ABOUT ORPHEUS

The Greco-Roman myth of Orpheus, an allegory of grief, has roots in Ovid's *Metamorphoses* and Virgil's *Georgics*. Orpheus was not a god but a hero who lived, suffered, and died. In some versions of the story he is struck by a thunderbolt hurled by Zeus, the ruler of the gods, who is angered by Orpheus' teaching of things unknown. In another, his countrymen dislike his teachings and conspire against him. One version has the women of Thrace tearing him in pieces because, after Eurydice's death, Orpheus neglects all women, teaches homosexuality, and condemns the promiscuity of the Maenads, thus angering the god Dionysus.

■

According to the myth, Orpheus' body was buried at Libethra in a tomb over which nightingales continually sang. The tomb, which actually exists, was considered a sacred place, and a cult developed around him. Orpheus became accepted as a mortal religious teacher whose doctrine was communicated in writings, "Orphics," attributed to him. In the sixth century B.C., this religion was established throughout southern Italy and in Sicily.

■

The Orpheus myth includes themes and motifs common to the folk tradition: conjugal devotion, journeys into unknown realms, and the taboo of looking back. The metamorphosis of Orpheus' lyre into a constellation of stars is the sort of transformation that often symbolizes a dispersal of all shadows of mourning, a conclusive banishment of grief, a happy ending.

■

Since its first telling, the myth has inspired musicians, poets, artists, and, later, filmmakers. In the seventeenth and eighteenth centuries, operatic versions of the story were composed by Claudio Monteverdi, Luigi Rossi, Christoph Willibald Gluck, and Franz Joseph Haydn. In 1858 Jacques Offenbach produced *Orphée aux enfers,* and in 1926 *Les Malheurs d'Orphée* by Darius Milhaud appeared. The poet Rainer Maria Rilke's *Sonnets to Orpheus* (1923) are a lyric celebration of the Orpheus legend, and in 1948 George Balanchine was inspired to choreograph a ballet to music by Igor Stravinsky. Recent tellings that incorporate or use the Orpheus themes include the plays by Jean Anouilh, *Eurydice* (1942), and Tennessee Williams, *Orpheus Descending* (1957). In films, the story was transposed to contemporary France by Jean Cocteau, in *Orphée* (1950), and to Rio de Janeiro during carnival by Marcel Camus in *Black Orpheus* (1958).

■

Perhaps because Orpheus was a musician, he has been a popular subject for people in the arts. Among painters who have used the Orpheus and Eurydice theme have been il Padovanino in "Bouttas Showing Orpheus Enchanting the Animals"; Titian, "Orpheus and Eurydice"; Jean Delville, "Orphée"; John Macallan Swan, "Orpheus"; Corot, "Orpheus Leading Eurydice from the Underworld"; Poussin, "Orphée et Euridice"; and Odilon Redon and Gustave Moreau. The sculptor Auguste Rodin also made several sculptures and drawings on the subject of Orpheus.

BIBLIOGRAPHY

Baumgarten, Fritz. *Die Hellenische Kultur.* Leipzig: Druck and Verlag von B. G. Teubner, 1905.

Coolidge, Olivia. *Greek Myths.* Boston: Houghton Mifflin, 1964.

Grant, Michael and John Hazel. *Gods and Mortals in Classical Mythology.* Springfield: G. & C. Merriam, 1973.

Graves, Robert. *The Greek Myths: Vol. I.* London: Penguin, 1955.

Kingsley, Charles. *The Heroes.* New York: Macmillan, 1954.

Larousse Encyclopedia of Mythology. London: Paul Hamlyn, 1959.

Oswalt, Sabine. *Greek and Roman Mythology.* Glasgow: Collins, 1969.

Patric, Richard and Peter Cross. *Classic Ancient Mythology.* London: Galley Press, 1987.

Tappan, Eva. *Stories from the Classics.* Boston: Houghton Mifflin, 1907.

DISCOGRAPHY

Clerambault, Louis-Nicholas. *Orphée* (1728). Harmonia Mundi HMC 901329.

Gluck, Christoph Willibald. *Orfeo ed Euridice* (1762). London 417 410–2.

Haydn, Franz Joseph. *Orfeo ed Euridice* (1791). Myto 2 MCD 905.29.

Milhaud, Darius. *Les Malheurs d'Orphée* (1927). Ades 13.284.2.

Monteverdi, Claudio. *L'Orfeo* (1607). Archive 419 250–2.

Rossi, Luigi. *Orfeo* (1647). Harmonia Mundi HMC 901358.60.

Thanks to Steve, Tatiana, and of course, Carole. — C.M.